Contents

KU-541-790

Look for these boxes:

Stay safe
These boxes tell you how to keep yourself and your friends safe from harm.

In your day
These boxes show you how science is a part of your daily life.

Measure up!
These boxes give you some fun facts and figures to think about.

Some words appear in bold, **like this**. You can find out what they mean by looking at the green bar at the bottom of the page or in the glossary.

Seeing things

Think about how you are reading the words on this page. You can read these words because your eyes can see. Seeing things helps us find out about the world around us.

The sense of sight

We have five **senses** to help us understand our world. They are sight, smell, touch, hearing, and taste. Sight is very important. It shows us sizes, shapes, and colours. It tells us where we are going and how far away things are. It helps us read, play, learn, watch things, and more.

Light and dark

We can see when it is light, but not so well when it is dark. When we go into a room with no lights or windows, it is dark. The room and the things in it look black because there is no light to help us see them.

In your day

Just because you cannot see things, it does not mean they are not there. When you are walking around in the dark, make sure you go slowly or you will bump into things!

senses   five ways in which our bodies find out about the world

3/13

BRO

T

S

Books should be returned or renewed by the last date above. Renew by phone **08458 247 200** or online *www.kent.gov.uk/libs*

Libraries & Archives

CUSTOMER SERVICE EXCELLENCE
UK
The Government Standard

Kent County Council

Louise Spilsbury

C333277114

www.raintreepublishers.co.uk
Visit our website to find out more information about Raintree books.

To order:
☎ Phone 0845 6044371
📄 Fax +44 (0) 1865 312263
🖥 Email myorders@raintreepublishers.co.uk

Customers from outside the UK please telephone +44 1865 312262

Raintree is an imprint of Capstone Global Library Limited, a company incorporated in England and Wales having its registered office at 7 Pilgrim Street, London, EC4V 6LB – Registered company number: 6695582

Text © Capstone Global Library Limited 2012
First published in hardback in 2012
Paperback edition first published in 2013
The moral rights of the proprietor have been asserted.

All rights reserved. No part of this publication may be reproduced in any form or by any means (including photocopying or storing it in any medium by electronic means and whether or not transiently or incidentally to some other use of this publication) without the written permission of the copyright owner, except in accordance with the provisions of the Copyright, Designs, and Patents Act 1988 or under the terms of a licence issued by the Copyright Licensing Agency, Saffron House, 6–10 Kirby Street, London EC1N 8TS (www.cla.co.uk). Applications for the copyright owner's written permission should be addressed to the publisher.

Edited by Claire Throp, Megan Cotugno, and Vaarunika Dharmapala
Designed by Steve Mead
Original illustrations © Capstone Global Library Ltd 2012
Illustrations by Oxford Designers & Illustrators
Picture research by Ruth Blair
Originated by Capstone Global Library Ltd
Printed and bound in China by Leo Paper Products Ltd

ISBN 978 1 406 23413 8 (hardback)
16 15 14 13 12
10 9 8 7 6 5 4 3 2 1

ISBN 978 1 406 23419 0 (paperback)
17 16 15 14 13
10 9 8 7 6 5 4 3 2 1

British Library Cataloguing in Publication Data
Spilsbury, Louise
The science behind sight
612.8'4-dc22
A full catalogue record for this book is available from the British Library.

Acknowledgements
We would like to thank the following for permission to reproduce photographs: Corbis pp. **5** (© Radius Images), **6** (© LWA-Dann Tardif), **11** (© Rubberball), **16** (© Cecilia Enholm/Etsa), **22** (© Hans Neleman); Getty Images pp. **18** (Eric Raptosh Photography), **19** (Dan McCoy – Rainbow), **21** (David R. Tyner); Science Photo Library p. **25**; Shutterstock pp. **9** (© Tudor Catalin Gheorghe), **10** (© Sergey Dubrov), **11** (© Wallenrock), **13** (© Ana de Sousa), **17** (© Eric Isselée), **24** (© eprom).

Cover photograph reproduced with permission of Shutterstock (© Bo Valentino).

We would like to thank Nancy Harris for her invaluable help in the preparation of this book.

Every effort has been made to contact copyright holders of any material reproduced in this book. Any omissions will be rectified in subsequent printings if notice is given to the publisher.

All the internet addresses (URLs) given in this book were valid at the time of going to press. However, due to the dynamic nature of the internet, some addresses may have changed, or sites may have changed or ceased to exist since publication. While the author and publisher regret any inconvenience this may cause readers, no responsibility for any such changes can be accepted by either the author or the publisher.

Light and sight

When it is dark at bedtime and you want to read, you turn your lamp on. We use light from lamps to see when it is dark.

Luminous things

Things that give off light are **luminous**. The Sun is luminous. We use light from the Sun to see things during the day. Lamps, fires, televisions, and torches are luminous, too.

Do you think this boy could read his book without using a torch?

luminous object that produces light

In your day

Shadows happen when something stops light moving through it. Stand outside on a sunny day. Are there trees nearby? Can you see shadows under them?

Making shadows

Light from luminous objects travels in straight lines. It can move through clear things such as air, water, and glass. That is how windows let light inside our homes so we can see. We say clear things are **transparent**. If you pull curtains across a window, you stop light getting inside. The curtains are **opaque**. Opaque things do not let light through.

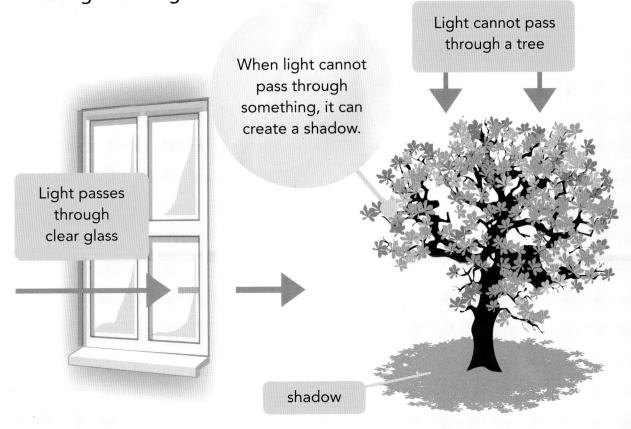

Light cannot pass through a tree

When light cannot pass through something, it can create a shadow.

Light passes through clear glass

shadow

transparent	object that you can see through
opaque	object that you cannot see through

Reflecting light

We see luminous objects because they give off light.
However, most things we see are not luminous. Tables,
chairs, footballs, and fields do not give off light. Instead,
they **reflect** it! Light bounces off surfaces and objects
around us, and we see them when some of that
reflected light enters our eyes.

light

We see things when
they give off light or
when light bounces
off them.

In your day

Bounce a ball. Notice how the ball bounces off in different
directions each time. When light reflects off a surface, it
changes direction, too.

reflect   bounce back light

More light, more sight

We can see better when it is lighter. When you are in a dark room, a candle **illuminates** only a small area. If you turn on a ceiling light, it lights up the whole room. Some surfaces reflect light better than others. Black fabric does not reflect light well. Light reflects best off shiny surfaces, such as mirrors.

Stay safe

When you and your family are out at night, remember to carry a torch and wear light-coloured clothing and a reflective strip. Reflective strips reflect light so that drivers can see you.

A candle only lights a small space. If you want more light you have to light more candles.

illuminate   shine light on something

How eyes work

An eye is shaped like a round ball. Most of it is inside your head. Do you know what the outer parts of the eye – the parts that you can see – do?

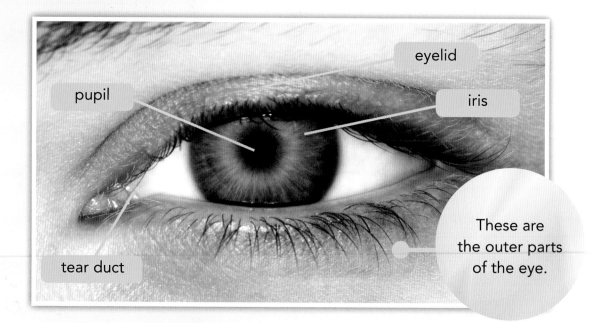

eyelid

pupil

iris

tear duct

These are the outer parts of the eye.

Eye care

Eyelids can close quickly to protect your eyes. When an eyelid **blinks**, it washes the surface of the eye with tears. Tears wash dust and other things off the eye. Tears leave your eye through a tiny tube called a **tear duct**.

> **Measure up!**
> Most people blink around 12 times every minute! Can you work out how many times we blink in an hour?

blink   close and open the eyelids quickly
tear duct   tiny tube through which tears leave the eye

Letting in light

The coloured part of your eye is the **iris**. The black spot in the middle of the iris is an opening called the **pupil**. The pupil lets light into the eye. In bright light your eye needs to take in less light, so the pupil becomes smaller. In low light, the pupil becomes bigger to take in more light.

Your pupil changes size to control how much light enters your eye.

In your day

Look at your eyes in a mirror and then close them. Open them quickly to see your pupils get smaller in bright light.

iris round, coloured part of the eye
pupil opening in the centre of the iris that appears to be black

Light and lenses

Light passes into the eye through a **lens**. A lens works a bit like a magnifying glass. When you look through a magnifying glass it makes things very clear.

In the same way, the lens **focuses** light so the image that we see is clear. It focuses the image on to the **retina**. The retina is the surface at the back of the eyeball. The image that the lens sends to the retina is upside down. The brain turns it the right way up so we know what we are looking at!

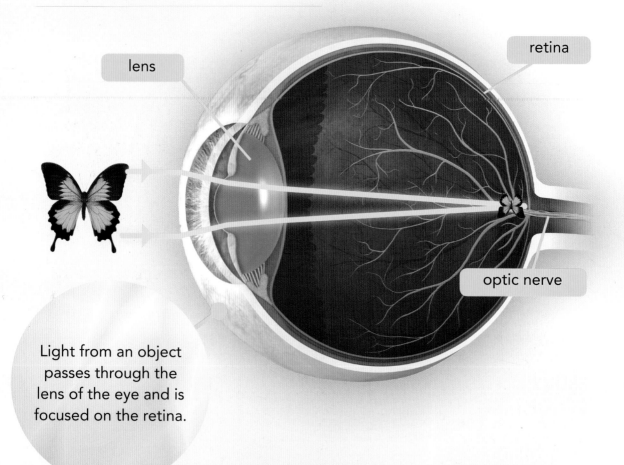

lens

retina

optic nerve

Light from an object passes through the lens of the eye and is focused on the retina.

lens	part of the eye which lets in light
focus	look at something in a way that makes it clear

Messages to the brain

When you want to send a message to a friend, you text them. The retina sends messages about what your eyes see to the brain. First it changes the colours and shapes in the image into millions of signals. Then it sends these signals to the brain along a pathway called the **optic nerve**. The brain works out what the signals mean.

When you look at things far away, the lens in your eye changes shape.

In your day

Look away from this book and focus on something far away. You will not feel it, but the shape of your lenses changes. The lens becomes thinner when the eye looks at things close-up. It becomes thicker when the eye looks at things far away.

retina   surface at the back of the eyeball
optic nerve   pathway from the eye to the brain

Animal sight

Some animals see the world in a different way from us. Our eyes are on the front of our heads. Rabbits and horses have eyes on the sides of their heads. What is the difference?

Eyes at the front

Close one eye and try to touch the ends of two pencils together. Why is it so hard? With only one eye, you cannot judge exactly how far away things are. With two eyes at the front, each eye sees a slightly different view. The brain compares the two views to work out exactly how far away something is and how fast it is moving.

Foxes, lions, and most other predators (animals who hunt other animals) have two eyes on the front of their head, like us. This helps them to hunt and catch animals.

In your day

You cannot judge distance very well with just one eye. Try playing with a ball with one eye shut. You will find that you are more likely to get hit by the ball than catch it! Take care not to hurt yourself!

Eyes at the side

Animals with one eye on each side of their head can see when a predator comes up behind them. The downside is that the two eyes work separately. Because the images that the eyes see are so different, the brain cannot compare them to work out exactly how far away things are.

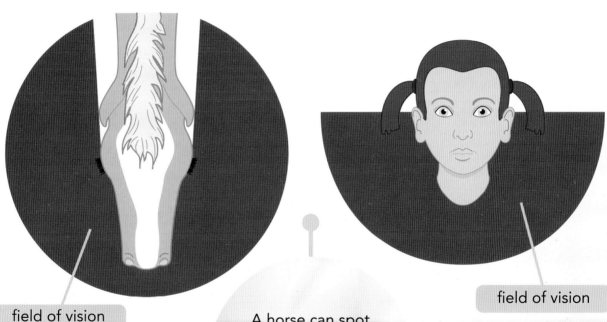

field of vision

A horse can spot things moving on all sides. Our eyes see what is straight ahead of us.

field of vision

Seeing at night

A cat's eyes glow in the dark because they have a part behind their **retinas** that works a bit like a mirror. It **reflects** light back on to the retina. Because more light is reflected on to the retina, the cat can see more. That is why cats and some other animals can see better in low light than we can.

Have you ever wondered why a cat's eyes glow in the dark?

In your day

The person who invented road reflectors got the idea from cat's eyes! Reflectors on roads reflect light from car headlamps. They help drivers see where their lane is.

Pupil power

To let more light into your room, you open the curtains wide. When it is nearly dark, cats' **pupils** open very wide to let as much light in as possible. In bright light, their pupils are very narrow. This stops their retinas from being hurt by too much light.

Can you tell which of these cats is looking into bright light and which is looking into low light?

Stay safe

Your pupils get smaller if you look into bright light. This protects your retinas. However, sunlight can still damage your retinas. Wear sunglasses and a hat to cover yourself up during summer.

Wearing glasses

People wear glasses to help them see clearly. People who are short-sighted can see things close by clearly, but things further away look blurry. People who are long-sighted can see things that are far away clearly, but things up close look blurry. Wearing glasses helps these people to see better.

Stay safe

An **optician** is someone who checks people's sight. An optician will ask you to read things close up and look at things far away to see if you have any sight problems.

Glasses help some people to see better.

optician   person who tests people's eyes to see if they need glasses

In your day
Put a straw in a glass of water and look at it from the side. At certain angles, the straw looks broken. That is because the water in the glass bends light as you are looking at it. Bending light is called refraction.

Why do people need glasses?

The **lens** in your eye **refracts** light to **focus** it on the **retina**. Sight problems happen when a person's lens does not refract light on to the retina properly.

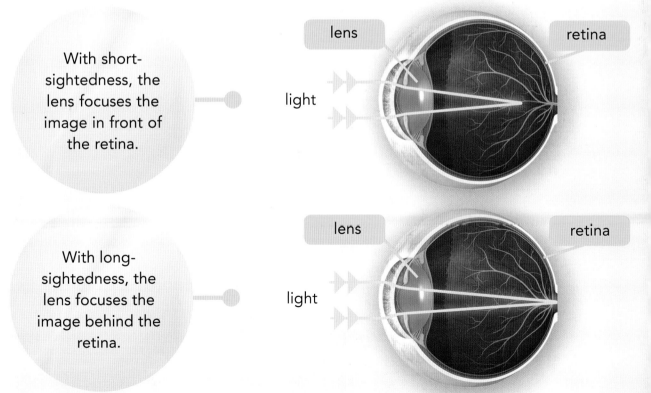

With short-sightedness, the lens focuses the image in front of the retina.

lens

retina

light

With long-sightedness, the lens focuses the image behind the retina.

lens

retina

light

refract   bend light

How glasses work

Glasses and contact lenses work by refraction. Lenses in glasses are made from pieces of **transparent** plastic or glass. The pieces are curved so the lenses can bend light. Lenses bend light to focus it on the right spot on the retina. This allows the wearer to see clearly.

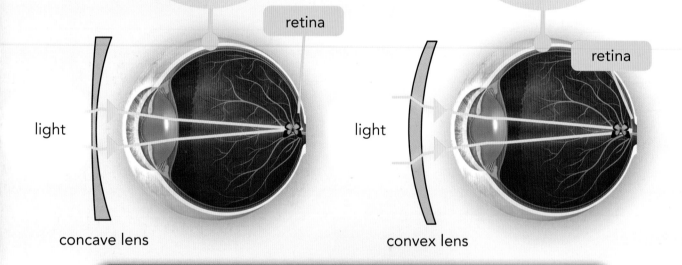

Concave lenses bend light outwards to help the lens focus the image on the retina.

Convex lenses bend light inwards to help the lens focus the image on the retina.

retina

retina

light

light

concave lens

convex lens

In your day

Lay a piece of cling film over a newspaper. Put a droplet of water on to the cling film. The curved blob of water should refract light and make the letters on the newspaper look bigger. You have made a lens!

Stay safe

Your eyes are precious. Fast-moving balls can damage eyes so be careful when playing racket sports. Take breaks from computers and games consoles so your eyes do not become tired out.

What are contact lenses?

Contact lenses work in the same way as lenses in a pair of glasses. They are tiny curved lenses that fit on to the eyeball itself. Tears on the surface of the eye help to hold the contact lenses in place. Contact lenses are very thin and small, so wearers say they cannot feel them.

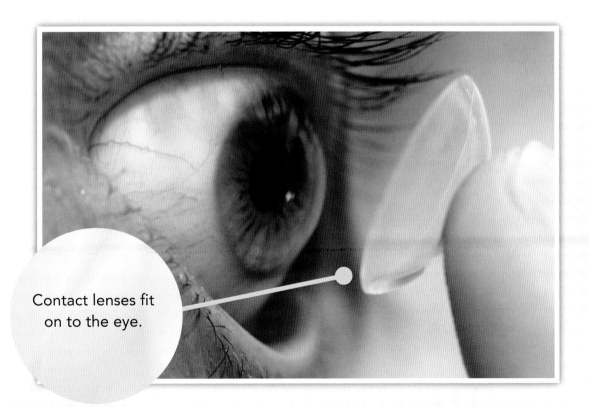

Contact lenses fit on to the eye.

Seeing more

Have you ever used a magnifying glass to look at insects? Magnifying things makes them look bigger so you can see them in detail.

You need binoculars to look at something really far away, such as a bird in the sky. Binoculars have two **lenses** for each eye, one in front of the other. The first lens **focuses** light from the faraway object to make an image. The second lens magnifies the image.

Have you ever used binoculars to see things that are far away?

How can you see over walls?

You can use bent light to see over things, such as walls and fences, or to look around corners! A **periscope** is a long tube with two mirrors inside – one at the top and the other at the bottom. The mirrors are placed at angles. When light from the outside hits the top mirror it **reflects** to the lower mirror. Then the light reflects into a person's eye so they can see the image from the top mirror.

Stay safe

Never look directly at the Sun, especially through binoculars. Binoculars magnify light. Looking at the Sun through them is very dangerous for your eyes.

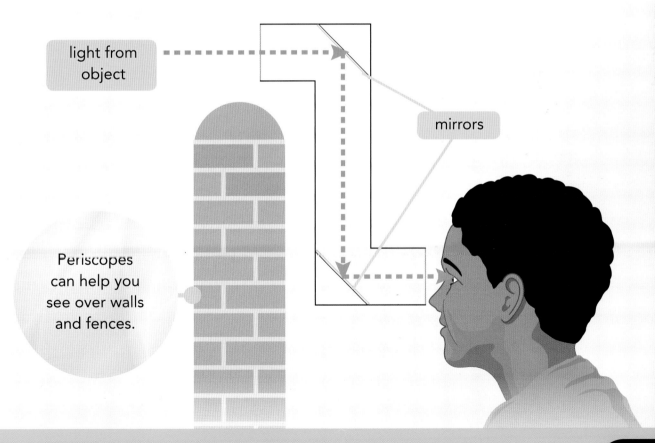

light from object

mirrors

Periscopes can help you see over walls and fences.

---

periscope   device that lets you look around walls, corners, or other obstacles

Sight and the brain

When you were born, your eyes were three-quarters the size of an adult's eyes. At first, you could only see things close up. Everything else was blurry.

For the first two months or so, your eyes did not work together. Sometimes you may have looked cross-eyed. Your eyes had to **focus** to see clearly. Your brain had to learn to see things the right way up and to use your two eyes together to judge distances.

As babies explore their world, their brains learn to make sense of what they see around them.

Can you believe your eyes?

Your brain and eyes work together to create images that make sense of our world. Sometimes you can trick your brain! **Optical illusions** are images that trick the brain into seeing things that are not there. Optical illusions work because the brain is trying to understand what we see. It uses rules that it has learned in the past to work out the images the eyes send it. Try this one!

In this optical illusion, all the lines going across the picture are straight. Your brain is tricked into thinking they are not straight because the black and white blocks are not lined up.

optical illusion   something that tricks your eyes into seeing something that is not there

Try it yourself

Make a pinhole camera.

What you need

- clean, empty crisps tube with a plastic lid
- scissors
- drawing pin
- greaseproof paper
- sticky tape
- kitchen foil

What to do

1. Ask an adult to cut 5 centimetres (2 inches) off the bottom of the tube. Then use a drawing pin to make a tiny hole in the centre of the bottom of this short piece. This is like the **pupil** of your eye – it is a little hole to let in light.

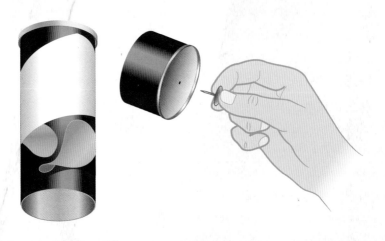

2. The plastic lid at the other end of the tube will be like your **retina** – this is the part the image will hit. Put a piece of greaseproof paper over the lid. Then put the lid on to the short piece of tube. Put the longer piece back on top and tape these pieces together.

plastic lid

3. To keep light out of the tube, wrap a piece of kitchen foil twice around the tube and attach it using sticky tape.

4. Outside on a sunny day, close one eye and hold the open end of the tube to your other eye. Do not look directly at the Sun! Keep the inside dark by holding your hands around the end of the tube by your eye.

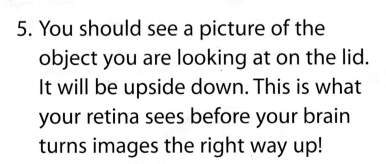

5. You should see a picture of the object you are looking at on the lid. It will be upside down. This is what your retina sees before your brain turns images the right way up!

Glossary

blink close and open the eyelids quickly

focus look at something in a way that makes it clear

illuminate shine light on something

iris round, coloured part of the eye

lens part of the eye that lets in light

luminous object that produces light

opaque object that you cannot see through

optical illusion something that tricks your eyes into seeing something that is not there

optician person who tests people's eyes to see if they need glasses

optic nerve pathway from the eye to the brain

periscope device that lets you look around walls, corners, or other obstacles

pupil opening in the centre of the iris that appears to be black

reflect bounce back light

refract bend light

retina surface at the back of the eyeball

senses five ways in which our bodies find out about the world

tear duct tiny tube through which tears leave the eye

transparent object that you can see through

Find out more

Use these resources to find more fun and useful information about the science behind sight.

Books

Light and Dark (Ways Into Science), Peter Riley (Franklin Watts, 2008)

Seeing (The Five Senses), Rebecca Rissman (Raintree, 2011)

Sight (Our Five Senses), Sally Morgan (Wayland, 2009)

Vision Without Sight (Shockwave), Susan Brocker (Scholastic, 2009)

Why Do I Need Glasses? (Inside My Body), Carol Ballard (Raintree, 2011)

Websites

www.childrensuniversity.manchester.ac.uk/ interactives/science/brainandsenses/eye.asp
Visit this website to play a game that will help you remember the positions of many eye parts.

www.healthyeyes.org.uk/index.php?id=7
This website includes some fun optical illusions to try. It also gives you some great tips on looking after your eyes.

www.childrenfirst.nhs.uk/kids/health/ask_doc/g/ glasses.html
Find out all about wearing glasses on this website.

www.guidedogs.org.uk/helpus/children
Visit this website to find out how people who have problems with their sight can be helped by guide dogs.

Index